D0296394

THE ESSENTIAL CAT

Thomas Wester

Foreword by Doris Lessing

SOUVENIR PRESS

Copyright © 1985 by Thomas Wester
Foreword Copyright © 1985 by Doris Lessing
Translation Copyright © 1987 by Trevi Publishers

Originally published in Sweden by Trevi Publishers
under the title *Katter*
First British edition published 1987 by Souvenir Press Ltd,
43 Great Russell Street, London WC1B 3PA

ISBN 0 285 62820 8

Printed in Great Britain by
BAS Printers Limited, Over Wallop, Hampshire

Foreword

Cats – the mysterious and beautiful creatures who share our lives, if we are lucky – inspire many books. Books about cats proliferate. Cat books of every kind are published in hundreds every year. There are reminiscences of loved pets, biographies of outstanding and special cats – for cats differ in their qualities as much as people do – memoirs of people who have devoted their lives to rescuing strays and the abandoned. Many of these books are straightforward and sensible, and one may learn a great deal about cats from them. Naturalists increasingly study them, and come up with facts that demolish many of the wrong ideas some people have about cats – such as, that they are unfeeling, aloof, and prefer to be solitary. Cats often help each other when they are in trouble, live in groups when they can, develop friendships with each other, and quickly become attached to humans who are good to them. All of which, or course, was observed by the people who lived with them and liked them, before the scientists got round to it.

There are also a great many books of photographs about cats. For some reason, few of these are any good. Many are coy, devoted to the pretty kitty, the charming kitten. They are often facetious, self-consciously funny: on the whole disappointing. Most often, they are not about cats, but about people. Cats are photographed, and described, as if they are persons, with human characteristics. These are usually whimsical.

This book is not at all pretty, funny, or coy, nor are the cats seen as people. It is about cats. Cats of every kind, at home and abroad, stray cats, loved cats, cats at play and at rest, asleep and hunting.

These are very good photographs. Thomas Wester is a brilliant photographer. He has photographed the essence of Cat. Again and again, with these pictures, one is stopped by, seized by, recognition: yes, this is it, absolutely; yes, this is just right, exactly as it is: I have seen this pose, this look, a hundred times, but not as sharply and completely as it is shown here . . .

This is, quite simply, the best book of photographs of cats there is. I shall treasure it.

Doris Lessing

To Felicia

You must be wondering where this is. The cats live in an old house near
a lake in southern Sweden.

If you see Moses, the white cat, sitting on this doorstep, open the door (the code is 4896) and let him in. He will go and wait by the lift, to be taken up to his flat.

Break-out in the country.

If they can do it in the country, why don't I have a go, too?

Housecat on a lead taking a walk in the city.

After thirty seconds of mortal combat the rest of the cat colony moves
in to break it up.